What Animal is This?

Christine Lawrie

Illustrated by

Maggie Downer

Evans

I'll think of some animals.
See if you can guess what
they are.

What very small insect has a bright red shell with black spots? It lives in the garden.

Turn the page to find the answer.

The ladybird's shell covers its wings.

Gardeners like ladybirds. Ladybirds eat the insects that can damage garden plants.

Let's pretend we are on
the plains in Africa.

What huge animal has
big ears and a trunk?
It has tusks made of ivory.

Elephants are the biggest animals that live on land.

Elephants use their trunks to pick up food and to suck up water. They squirt the water into their mouths.

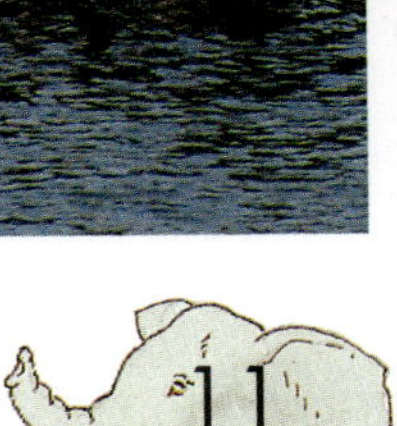

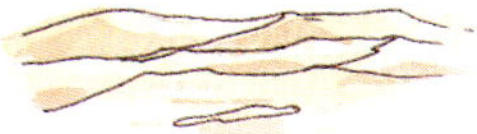
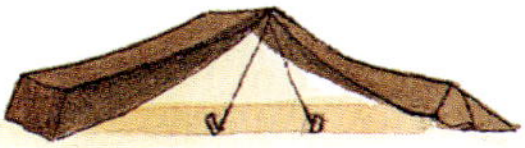

Now let's pretend we
are in the desert.

What animal has a
long neck and a hump
on its back?
It can go for a long time
without needing a drink.

People use camels to carry them across the desert.

Camels can live in hot, dry places. They store fat in their humps which can be turned into water.

Let's think of an animal that
lives in Australia.

What animal has a long tail, big hind legs and moves by jumping? It carries its baby in a pouch.

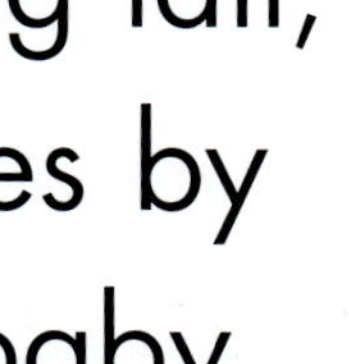

It can jump very fast.

A baby kangaroo is
called a joey.

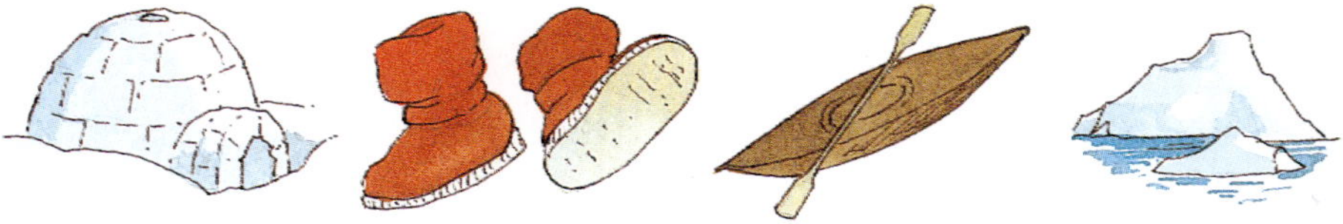

Let's go somewhere cold.
We can pretend to
be near the North Pole.

What animal is very big and has white fur? It hunts seals and fish.

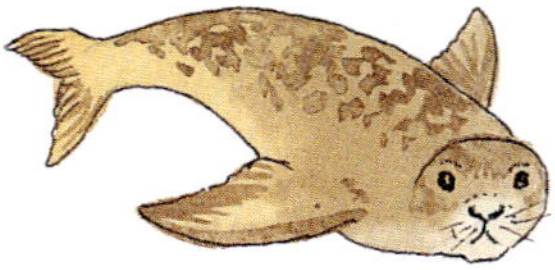

Polar bears are very good swimmers.

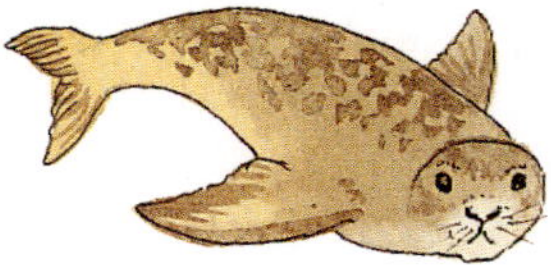

The cubs are born in winter in a den under the snow. In the spring they go hunting with their mother.

Let's pretend we
are in a rain forest.

What animal slithers through
the leaves and branches?
It is very long and has
no legs.

This snake is a boa constrictor. It lives in the rain forest in South America.

Boa constrictors squeeze animals to death. Then they swallow them whole.

Let's guess one more animal that we might find in the garden.

What has eight legs and spins a web to catch its food?

It eats flies and other insects that get stuck in the web.

Well done!